Soaring In

The Journey of an Origi

Granville Coggs, M.D. and Coggs Rowell

www.coggs-granville.com

Graphic Artist: Erik Swanson
Editor: Leslie McClinton

Cover image:
Granville Coggs at the Tuskegee Army Airfield in front of an AT-6 plane in 1945.

Soaring Inspiration

The Journey of an Original Tuskegee Airman

Granville Coggs, M.D. and
Anita Coggs Rowell

Dedication

This book is dedicated to every young person who must overcome an obstacle, impediment, or handicap in order to reach a goal and fulfill his destiny. I promise that if you work with integrity and persistence, you will exceed everyone's expectations. That's exactly what I did!

Acknowledgements

I would like to thank the following people:

Mrs. Maud Currie Coggs – for being a wonderful and supportive wife

Ms. Eloise Coggs – for providing many facts from her prodigious memory

Ms. Gina Valdez – for transcription and advice

Ms. Debbie Bernal – for conceiving of my delivery of Lincoln's Gettysburg Address and posting it on YouTube

Table of Contents

My Childhood

On a cold December morning in 1930, I asked my mother for one Christmas present, an A. C. Gilbert Chemistry set. Although I was five years old, I was determined to learn about mixtures and solutions. I would have asked for the chemistry set for my birthday, which is July 30th, but Christmas came sooner.

When T.W. heard about my request, he said, “Don’t give Gran a chemistry set because he’ll blow up the house.” T.W. stands for Tandy Washington and he is my brother, but what does he know?

Weewee put her hand on her hip and added, “Yeah, Peanut doesn’t have a drop of common sense, he’s all brains. There ain’t no telling what he’ll do with a bunch of chemicals.”

If Mother had not been standing there, I would have punched Weewee right in her stomach for saying that. She ain’t all that smart anyway!

I’ll get her next time.

Weewee is my sister and her real name is Eloise. She got that nickname from Dad. He calls Mother his “Big partner”, my sister Nanette is his “Little partner”, and Eloise is his “Wee partner.”

I also have another brother Louis, and he is the oldest. I am the youngest, so I guess that’s why everyone thinks they know what’s best for me.

1929 Family picture when I was 4 years old. I am in front of my father, Tandy Washington Coggs I. My sister Eloise is standing between my father and mother, Nannie Hinkle Coggs. Pictured from left to right on the back row is Louis, Tandy Washington (T. W.), and Nanette.

Playing in front of our playhouse located in the front yard. I was about 5 years old.

Playing with Elijah Wilson on the right

Mom interrupted T.W. and Weewee, "Don't worry about Gran. I know he will do alright."

She got me that chemistry set for Christmas and I was overjoyed. I didn't know it then, but my interest in chemistry and science would pave the way for me to become successful in my career as a radiologist and inventor.

A 1940s Gilbert chemistry set

My chemistry set was made by the AC Gilbert toy company. AC Gilbert was founded by Alfred Carlton Gilbert, who was a physician by training. He and a friend founded the Mysto Manufacturing Company which produced tools for professional magicians. A few years later, Gilbert and his friend ended their business relationship and Gilbert changed the name of the company from Mysto Manufacturing to the A.C. Gilbert Company. Instead of selling only magic paraphernalia, the A. C. Gilbert Company sold an assortment of educational toys like chemistry sets, microscopes, tool sets, and engineering sets.

Along with playing, mixing chemical solutions, and fighting with Weewee, I had a job at home. My job was to empty all the slop jars every morning before going to school. Slop jars are metal cans that were kept under our beds in case we had to use the bathroom at night. Since our home did not have indoor plumbing, we did not have a toilet and had to use an outhouse.

Slop jars were a convenience that kept us from going outside to the outhouse in the middle of the night. After all, there was no tellin' what kind of animal might be waiting for some fresh meat!

Since we did not have running water, I took baths in a large metal tub.

Every Saturday night each of us took a bath in the tub which was placed in the bathroom. Then on Sunday morning we went to Sunday

A typical slop jar.

school and church at St. Paul Baptist Church. When we returned home, our typical Sunday dinner consisted of fried chicken, creamed corn, beans, pound cake and homemade ice cream for dessert. We made ice cream by churning a milk and sugar mixture in an ice cream maker. Our cows provided the fresh milk.

St. Paul Missionary Baptist Church on Georgia Ave in Pine Bluff, Arkansas. I was baptized here at 11 years old.

Ice cream maker

Grandpa Tandy, my father's dad, lived with us and grew prize winning strawberries in the backyard. Sometimes we would water his strawberry patch. The strawberries were so red and plump, we wanted to eat all of them and Grandpa Tandy knew this. He told us that if he saw our hands go anywhere near our mouths, he'd give us a spanking. To get around this, we developed a technique for getting the strawberries into our mouths without putting our hands "anywhere near our mouths."

We'd balance a strawberry on our thumb and propel it into our mouth which was held wide open. Once the berry landed, the warm, sweet juice would flood our mouth. This made picking weeds and watering a delight.

Grandpa Tandy Calvin Coggs

Fights and More Fights

Since Weewee is 2 years older than me, she often treated me like her little boy. She was always telling me what to do and guiding me away from interesting things like the pond full of water and dynamite caps. There was a pond of water near my house and I would often put on my boots so I could find out how far into the water I could walk before the water flowed into the tops of my boots. Mother did not like that; however, my curiosity extended beyond the chemistry set to the great outdoors. After all Arkansas is called, "The Natural State," and I cannot think of a better place to explore.

The location of our house was ideal for making new discoveries. We lived nine miles outside of Pine Bluff, Arkansas and there were unusual things on the ground. I was compelled to explore the dynamite caps lying in an area of the woods but Mother told Weewee to keep an eye on me. Therefore, she felt justified in bossing me around and I felt justified in trying to get my way. To add insult to injury, I stuttered when I got upset or excited. Therefore, I couldn't even talk fast enough to tell my side of the story.

Family home

Family home

The land on which our home was located. From right to left: Our home is the structure on the far right. There were peach and plum trees on the left of the house.

One day Mother and Father got tired of us fighting and decided to send us away to live with different families. Weewee and I sat on the porch and began to argue about which family we would live with. The argument turned into a fight and we got in trouble for that also.

Even though we had many fights, I knew Weewee loved me because when the white boy named Todd picked on me, she jumped on him and beat him so long that Mother had to pull her off of him. Mother and Father never sent us away. They endured our arguments and tried to teach us how to get along.

Elementary School

From first to sixth grade, I attended the Training School on the campus of Arkansas AM&N College. This was a branch of the University of Arkansas. My favorite class was recess because I enjoyed going out to play. We had recess in the morning and afternoon. We played on see saws, with marbles, and horseshoes. In fifth grade I played touch football during recess.

A float from Arkansas AM & N College

When I was 10 years old, Weewee and I went to see *West Point of the Air*, filmed at Randolph Air Force Base in Texas. Wallace Beery was one of the stars in the movie. It showed me how white pilots were trained after finishing West Point Military Academy. While I was thrilled to see the planes and pilots, I never thought I could become a military pilot because I was black and the military did not accept blacks for training as

High School

I began high school in 1937 and attended Dunbar High School in Little Rock, Arkansas. Dunbar was the high school for black students. It would be seventeen more years before the United States Supreme Court ordered all public schools integrated in 1954 and twenty more years before the Little Rock Nine integrated Central High School in 1957.

I enjoyed my Chemistry and Physics classes. The teachers were surprised to see someone like me doing so well in those subjects because it was usually the light skinned kids who got the best grades. I had caramel brown skin, tightly coiled hair and eczema on my face. I knew some people thought I was ugly but that was their problem, not mine. I refused to let their low expectations define me because my mother and father told me that I could be anything I wanted in spite of the occasional asthma attacks which left me gasping for air.

My mother, Nannie Hinkle, was born in 1887 and attended high school at Arkansas Baptist College where she met my father, Tandy Washington Coggs. When she graduated from 12th grade, she returned to her hometown of Okolona, Arkansas and taught elementary school students in a public school for black children. My father was enamored with Mother and proposed marriage. They were married in 1914.

At 27 years old, Mother was older than the typical bride of

that era. Most women were married by the time they were 22 years old. Mother was also frail and was told by her doctor that she'd never have children. Since she managed to have five children, Mother knew something about beating the odds and instilled in us the strong belief that with God all things are possible.

Some of my high school teachers were exceptional. Miss Sue Cowan Morris was my homeroom and English teacher. She received a master's degree from the University of Chicago and encouraged excellence from her students. My physics teacher was Mr. Wilson. Although he spoke with a lisp, he was also a great teacher.

By the time I entered 12th grade, I decided to pursue a career in engineering. I went to the white high school to take the SAT. I asked the white test proctor, "Where should I sit?"

Since this was during the time of segregation in America, I knew that I could not take any available seat and I was not sure if there would be a special place for colored people.

He smirked. "Sit anywhere you want. You ain't gonna pass anyway."

I took a seat and focused on the test. Father taught me about the importance of focus when he told me stories of how he raised hogs to pay for his college tuition. Although the hogs died one year and he could not afford to pay his tuition, he did not let that stop him. He eventually went back to school and graduated as the valedictorian from Arkansas Baptist College in 1910.

I worked as hard as possible on that exam and after a few months I obtained the test results. I scored higher than all the other test takers in the room! That test proctor was wrong.

College Days and World War II

I applied to California Tech, MIT, and Howard University. MIT was my first choice but they did not accept me. Therefore, I attended Howard in the fall of 1943 as a pre-med and pre-engineering student. During this same time, the United States of America had been engaged in World War II for two years at this point.

World War II began on December 7, 1941 when the Japanese bombed Pearl Harbor. Pearl Harbor is a Hawaiian Island where the U. S. Pacific Fleet of battleships was located. The goal of the Japanese was to immobilize the U. S. Navy so Japan could conquer the Far East and Pacific. Sailors aboard their ships were relaxed and did not expect the attack. That day 2,403 people were killed and eight battleships were destroyed. As a result of the attack, America declared war on Japan and three days later Japan's allies, Germany and Italy, declared war on America. This was the beginning of World War II.

One significant difference between the First World War and the second was the technology used in World War II. Air planes and air strikes were major components of World War II. Other technology included the atomic bomb, radar, and missiles.

I received notification from the Little Rock, Arkansas draft board that I would be drafted in the near future. Therefore, I decided to volunteer for the all black United States Army Air Corps because I thought that if I waited to be drafted, I'd wind up in the infantry.

Tuskegee

I knew two people from Arkansas who received their pilot wings and second lieutenant gold bars at Tuskegee Army Airfield: Herbert Clark who was from Pine Bluff and Richard Caesar from Lake Village. They were given extensive media coverage in national Negro newspapers. I volunteered for the Army Air Corps was tested and qualified as an aviation cadet. As a result of Mr. Wilson's and Miss Morris' teaching in high school, I scored very high on the United States Aptitude Tests which the US Army Air Corps required of aviation cadet applicants.

I was accepted and scheduled for training as a bombardier. After a few months of college training at Tuskegee Institute, I was trained in a pre-flight status as a cadet at Tuskegee Army Air Field.

There was an Army Air Corps composed of white pilots who were fighting the Germans. At this time, blacks were not allowed to become fighter pilots because of the false belief that they were intellectually incapable of flying fighter planes. This type of racism was common in America. It was also wide spread; for example, Bessie Coleman had to learn to fly in France because of the prejudice in America. I was born on July 30, 1925, three years after she became America's first black licensed pilot.

Eleanor Roosevelt visited the Tuskegee Institute which was

training blacks to become civilian pilots. While at Tuskegee, Mrs. Roosevelt took a ride in the plane of Charles "Chief" Anderson, the head of the civilian flight program. When she returned to Washington, DC, she told her husband that blacks could indeed fly and that they should be trained to become military pilots. As a result, President Roosevelt ordered the Army to establish a separate training program for black military pilots. Mrs. Roosevelt was quite courageous like Mrs. Florence Harding, the wife of President Warren Harding; she was the first president's wife to fly in an airplane.

Bombardier Training

I was in training to become a member of the 477 Medium Bomber Group as a bombardier. When flying to a target during combat, the bombardier was an auxiliary gunner. He was equipped with a machine gun which was operated with both hands. The bombardier helped ensure that the plane was not attacked by enemy planes while flying to the target. However, before I could become a bombardier, I had to train as a gunner.

I was sent to Tyndal Army Air Field, in Panama City, Florida for training as an aerial gunner. I received my military badge as an aerial gunner in the fall of 1944.

After I received my aerial gunner's badge, I returned to Tuskegee Army Air Field where I waited for my assignment to bombardier training school. While at Tuskegee, I met Maud Currie, who was a scholar/athlete at Tuskegee Institute. Shortly after meeting Maud, I was sent to Midland Army Air Field in Midland, Texas for Bombardier Training.

I graduated as a Bombardier at Midland Army Airfield in January of 1945, Class 45A. The pictures of all graduating cadets were sent to hometown newspapers. Although pictures of white graduating cadets were printed in the Arkansas Gazette and Arkansas Democrat, my picture was not included. My father went to these newspapers and asked why my picture was not printed. They replied, "It is simply our policy not to print pictures of colored people in our newspaper."

In spite of the negative response from the newspaper, being black was beneficial. If I had been white, I would have been assigned as a bombardier on a B-29 bomber with the Army Air Corps in the Far East. At this point, the Army concluded their successful experimental flight program at Tuskegee and decided to form an all black medium bomber organization. Medium bomber planes are B-25's which have two engines, large bombers are B-17's and B-24's which have four engines, and fighter planes are single engine planes. I was preparing to fly medium bombers.

B-24

B-25

B-25

On a bomber plane there are pilots, navigators, bombardiers, and gunners. Pilots fly the plane, navigators tell them where to fly, bombardiers drop bombs over the targets, and gunners protect the plane against enemy fighter planes trying to destroy the bomber.
Since the Army Air Corps needed Negro pilots and I displayed the necessary aptitude for acceptance as a pilot trainee, I was sent directly from training as a bombardier at Midland Army Airfield to pilot training at Tuskegee.

The primary phase of pilot training was carried out by Tuskegee Institute at Moten Field in Tuskegee, Alabama. Basic and advanced phases of pilot training were carried out at Tuskegee Army Airfield, located approximately 10 miles from Tuskegee Institute.

After receiving training as military pilots, blacks were not sent into war because the Air Force didn't want anything to do with black pilots; therefore, the pilots were sent directly to train in Northern Africa and Southern Italy. As a result of their military success, the Army used them to protect the bombers flying to bomb Berlin. Planes flown by the black pilots were called "Red Tails" because of the red paint on the back of the plane. On these bombing runs, German fighter planes were shooting down the bombers. However, when Red Tails accompanied the bombers, they never lost any of their escorted planes to enemy fighter planes. Colonial Benjamin O. Davis nicknamed his plane, "By Request," because white pilots requested that he escort them on bombing missions.

In advanced training, I flew in the B-25 medium bomber. I received my wings as a multi- engine military pilot in October of 1945. My mother, her friend Mrs. Nichols, and Maud Currie, my girlfriend, attended my graduation ceremony at Tuskegee.

Since the war ended on September 2, 1945, I did not fly any combat missions. Nevertheless, I treasured the experience and the training I received.

My graduation class 45G from pilot training in October, 1945. I am the third person from the left in the third row.

Back to College

Following my graduation as a pilot in 1945, I applied to become a member of the Regular United States Army Air Corps. I was not selected for inclusion in the Regular Army Air Corps because I was a high school graduate who had not served in combat in Europe. Many of the earlier trained Tuskegee Airmen had graduate degrees and comprised the outstanding combat service of the 332nd Fighter Group.

I worked as a weather observer with the weather station at Tuskegee Army Airfield for about six months hoping to improve my chances of remaining in the Army Air Corps. I was wrong.

Since my girlfriend, Maud, was planning to attend the University of Nebraska, I decided to apply as well. I wanted to be her roommate. American culture was more conservative at this time and one did not live with someone of the opposite sex unless they were married. Therefore, I proposed to Maud and thankfully, she accepted my proposal. We got married August 20, 1946 and classes began the next month in September.

Maud had a scholarship from the General Education Board and was working on her master's degree in Nutrition Education. I paid for most of my education using the GI Bill. I worked as a waiter to help with other expenses. We rented a room from a local homeowner since the university did not allow blacks to live in the dorms or eat in the cafeteria.

Maud graduated with her master's degree in June, 1947. I graduated June, 1949 with a bachelor's of science degree in chemistry. I was in the top three percent of my class and was elected to the Phi Beta Kappa, Sigma Xi, and Phi Lambda Upsilon honor societies.

Harvard Medical School

I decided to become a doctor and was accepted into 11 of the 12 medical schools that I applied to. I chose to attend Harvard Medical School (HMS) which treated Black students with the respect we deserved as human beings. I did not take such treatment for granted. I was extremely grateful for the comfortable dining hall at Harvard because I had experienced the bitter reality of sleeping in separate quarters and eating at separate tables in the mess hall at Midland Army Airfield during my training as a Bombardier. Harvard treated me like a person.

The accommodating treatment did not lessen the academic rigors of medical school, however. Since I graduated with distinct honors from the University of Nebraska, I felt certain that I could handle my classes at Harvard. I confidently wore my Phi Beta Kappa pin to class until I received my grade from the first anatomy exam which was a D. The assistant dean of students took me to the side and told me I had to do better if I expected to graduate from HMS. Since many of my classmates attended Harvard College before coming to HMS, they were used to essay questions. I, on the other hand was accustomed to multiple choice questions on exams and there is a big difference! Once I learned to study for those essay questions, my performance improved. That reality check was just the motivation I needed to buckle down and work harder. I also took that Phi Beta Kappa pin off and placed it in my dresser.

I graduated from HMS in June, 1953. When one graduates from medical school, he cannot begin to immediately practice medicine. Medical school graduates have to choose a specialty and become trained in a particular field of medicine. This extra training is called a residency. Some examples of well-known medical specialties are family medicine, pediatrics, and emergency medicine. I decided to specialize in radiology. Radiology is the study of x-rays for the purpose of diagnosing and treating diseases. I chose radiology because I was impressed with the quality of life I observed among other radiologists. I completed my residency at the University of California Hospital in San Francisco, June, 1958.

My siblings also completed their college and post graduate education by this time. Louis, my oldest brother, was a doctor specializing in family medicine. T.W. became a pastor. Nanette was trained as a medical technologist; however, she decided to become a reading specialist with the Chicago public schools and Weewee, Eloise, became a psychiatric social worker.

My Career as a Radiologist

As a radiologist, I was keenly aware of the need for an early diagnosis of cancer. Betty Ford, President Gerald Ford's wife, and Happy Rockefeller, Nelson Rockefeller's wife, changed the culture of secrecy regarding breast cancer. In 1974, both of these women publically disclosed their breast cancer diagnosis. Before that time, women suffered in silence and fear. Ford and Rockefeller made it socially acceptable to reveal a breast cancer diagnosis. At this time, I was a full-time faculty member at the University of California in San Francisco in charge of mammography. I was encouraged because I realized that encouraging women to obtain mammograms was something I could do to help save lives. In addition I educated women about the benefits of early detection.

A few highlights of my medical career:

1958 - First black physician on staff at Kaiser Foundation Hospital in San Francisco

1964 - Scientific Exhibit, "Intravenous Aortic Study," 7th International Neuroradiological Symposium at the Waldorf Astoria Hotel in New York. An intravenous aortic study occurs when a substance is injected into the veins for the purpose of studying details of the aorta, which is the main artery in the heart.

1972 - Established the first ultrasound division at UC San Francisco

1983 - Presentation at the Annual Meeting of the Radiological Society of North America, "The Efficacy of a Community Based Multi-Modality Breast Diagnostic Center." This was a presentation to demonstrate how a breast diagnostic center is effective by using different procedures to detect if cancer is present. These procedures include: mammography, which uses x-rays; ultrasound, which uses sound waves; thermography, which analyzes body temperature; and diaphanography, which uses a light source.

1983 - Established the San Antonio Breast Evaluation Center based on the multi-modality format of diagnosing breast cancer

1991 - Received patent for the Precision Breast Legion Localizer

1993 - Inventor of the "Central X-ray Beam Guided Breast Biopsy System." This biopsy system is designed to facilitate the performance of precise, accurate breast biopsies. A biopsy is the removal and examination of tissue from a living person to see if a disease is present.

Physical Fitness

In 1994, I was working five days a week in Kennedy, TX which is 67 miles from my house. The long drive was difficult and I had trouble staying awake. My journey to achieve the physical fitness of a senior age runner began with an idea from my brilliant wife, Maud. She thought that if I was in better physical condition, I would not have to stop to take a nap while on the road.

During the week, Maud and I ran in the dark, early mornings of our San Antonio neighborhood before I drove to work. On the weekends, we ran at the athletic field of the University of Texas Health Science Center. This was during daylight hours so there were other people exercising. After several months passed, I began to enjoy running and decided to train for track and field competitions.

Significant Running Medals

2010 - 3 gold medals in the 400M, 200M, and 100M events at the San Antonio Senior Games.

2011 - 3 gold medals in the 400M, 200M, and 100M events at the San Antonio Senior Games.

My wife, Maud Currie Coggs

I have not always maintained a healthy lifestyle. When I began working at Kaiser Permanente in San Francisco I stocked ice cream in my freezer. My favorite flavor was vanilla, but I also enjoyed other flavors. Today, however, there are no desserts in my house and when we go out to eat, I only eat dessert on special occasions.

My father lived to be 105 years old. I believe I have a great chance to live a long life also. Therefore, I eat healthy meals, exercise, and try to relax because I have learned that not running my motor at full speed all of the time is crucial to longevity.

My typical menu consists of the following:

Breakfast – Sandwich with one slice of whole wheat bread and fat free cheese, banana, grapes, and a cup of coffee with non-calorie sweetener.

Brunch - Frozen, low-calorie dinner with 230 calories or less like sweet and sour chicken.

Dinner - Orange juice with Metamucil, spinach salad with dressing, roma tomato, and half a can of tuna fish.

Midnight snack - raisin bran with seven prunes, non-calorie sweetener, diced peaches and a full bowl of fruit which includes pineapple chunks, honeydew melon, cantaloupe, and water melon.

Snacks - Red grapes are part of my therapeutic regimen. They move things along and keep me regular.

Running in a race

After a race with friends, March 2007

At home with my gold medal from the 1997 Senior Olympics for the 1500 Meter run. My time was 8:08.

My Exercise schedule:

- I ride my bike for 20 minutes outside or inside

- Stretch for 15 minutes

- Walk one loop around the cul de sac near my home which is approximately 300 meters and then I sprint one loop.

- Swim in 94 degree water for 30 minutes. I wear a life vest.
    - 10 slow laps on my back
    - 3 fast laps on my back
    - One fast lap freestyle

I work out like this because I am a senior athlete and it takes daily training to stay fit.

Mental Fitness

To maintain mental fitness I challenge my mind with music and memorization. I have played the gut bucket since 1956. This was given to me by my HMS classmate, Walter Coulson. He played the piano, trumpet, harmonica, and the gut bucket. One evening, he brought a gut bucket to a party and when he saw my enthusiasm, he gave me one. I have also played the flute, the electric bass guitar, and sung with the San Antonio Master Singers.

I recently memorized President Abraham Lincoln's Gettysburg Address. The Gettysburg Address is one of the most well-known speeches in the history of America. It was delivered during the Civil War four and a half months after the Union Army defeated the Confederate Army at the Battle of Gettysburg. I decided to memorize it for the challenge of testing my memory and I have recited it during several speaking engagements.

Playing the gut bucket at San Antonio Academy

Plan for Longevity

1. Select Long Lived Parents

2. Aerobic Activity

3. Eat Healthfully: High Fiber, Low Calorie, Low Fat

4. Vitamin and Mineral Supplements

5. Don't Do Drugs: Hard Drugs, Cigarettes, Alcohol

6. Married

7. Have a Sense of Humor

8. Get Enough Sleep

9. Wear Seat Belts and Shoulder Straps

10. Cancer Screening Procedures: Mammography, Colonoscopy, PSA Examinations

Significant Events and Awards

1943 – 1946 - I was awarded the following military badges from the U. S. Army Air Corps:

- o Aerial Gunner – 50 Caliber Machine Gun
- o Aerial Bombardier – Norden Bombsight
- o Pilot, Multi – Engine- B-25 Medium Bomber

1945 - Wings as a military pilot

1946 - Married Maud Currie

1953 - Granville Currie Coggs, my son, was born

1954 - Anita Marie Coggs, my first daughter, was born

1960 - Granville Currie Coggs died in an accident

1961 - Carolyn Anne Coggs, my second daughter, was born

2001 - Inducted into the Arkansas Black Hall of Fame

2003 - Keynote speaker at a Tuskegee Airman Educational Assistance banquet in the Officer's Club at Randolph Air Force Base

2007 - Congressional gold medal was presented to the Tuskegee Airmen in a special ceremony at the Capitol. President Bush saluted the Tuskegee Airmen at this ceremony. I was one of 300 original airmen who returned his salute.

2010 - Participated in the 2010 Pasadena Rose Bowl Parade along with 15 other original Tuskegee Airmen.

I am holding my newborn daughter, Anita, and my son Granville is looking at her, 1954

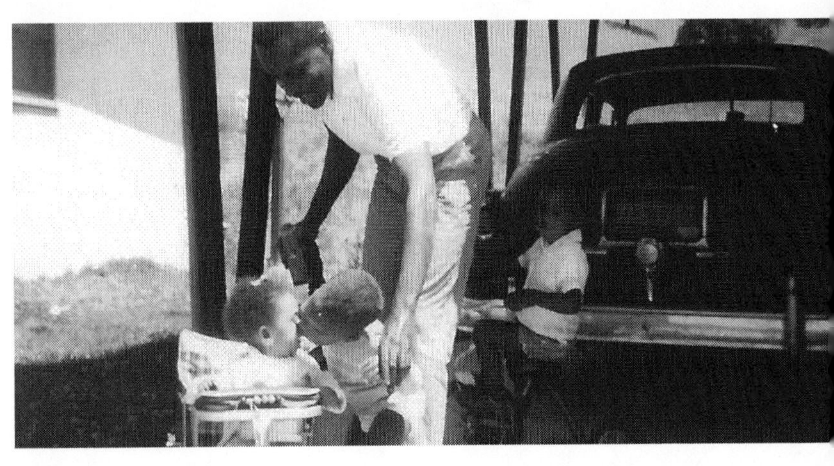

I am watching the children play. Granville is kissing Anita and a neighborhood friend is riding his tricycle, 1955

Maud is kissing Granville and Anita is in her walker, 1955

Granville, Maud, and Anita in the backyard

Anita, Maud, and Granville at Yosemite National Park

Anita, myself, and Granville with the Golden Gate Bridge in the background

My mother, Nannie Hinkle Coggs with Anita, 1961

Anita holding Carolyn, February, 1961

Carolyn and Anita

Anita and Carolyn

I am among 300 Tuskegee Airmen at the U. S. Capitol after the presentation of the Congressional Gold Medal by President George W. Bush, March 2007

Anita, Senator Blanche Lincoln, Maud, and myself in Senator Lincoln's office

Anita and myself in Senator Lincoln's office

With Senator Kay Bailey Hutchison, Maud, and Anita

Maud, Anita, and myself in Washington, DC March, 2007

Anita, Maud, Congressman Charles Gonzalez of the 20th Congressional District in San Antonio, Texas, and myself

The Trip of a Lifetime: President Obama's Inauguration

President Obama invited all original Tuskegee Airman to his inauguration ceremony. The San Antonio Express Newspaper printed a picture of John (Mule) Miles and I on the front page. I was impressed and exhilarated. 64 years earlier, I recalled the disappointment of not being recognized in the local newspapers of my hometown in Arkansas. Times do change.

The following is an account of the exhilarating experience I had at President Obama's inauguration written by my daughter, Anita Coggs Rowell:

The Trip of a Lifetime:

Traveling With My Father to the Presidential Inauguration of Barack Obama

It may as well have fallen out of the sky and dropped into my lap. That's how I felt about the opportunity to attend the Presidential Inauguration of Barack Obama.

This story began one afternoon in December, 2008, when I was listening to the 12 o'clock news on KTVU. The TV was on, but I wasn't paying a lot of attention. I was busy fixing a sandwich in the kitchen, and our television set is in the family room. So, I didn't catch the beginning of the piece, but I did hear, "…Diane Feinstein…Inauguration Committee… Tuskegee Airmen invited to the Presidential Inauguration of Barack Obama…."

I stopped what I was doing right there, so I could hear better, but the segment was over.

"What?" I thought. "Did I hear that right?" I knew I had, but for a moment it seemed surreal.

That meant that my father and other Tuskegee Airmen would be going to Washington, D.C. next month for the Inaugural Ceremony--as invited guests!

"That is so cool," I said to myself.

Soon after, I called my father, Dr. Granville Coggs, who lives in San Antonio, Texas.

"I heard the news on TV," I said. "That's great. Congratulations!"

"I know! I just got the word from our local Tuskegee Airmen chapter," he exclaimed. "I can hardly believe it myself!"

"Have they given you any more details?" I asked.

"No. Not yet. I'm sure we'll know more as soon as we hear from TAI." (Tuskegee Airmen, Inc.—the national organization).

"Great. Keep me posted."

Our conversation reminded me of when my mother, Maud Coggs, called my Aunt Baby, (her sister Zenobia Pendleton), two years ago to tell her that the Tuskegee Airmen would be receiving the Congressional Gold Medal at the Capitol in Washington, D.C.

My mom told me, "At first Aunt Baby didn't say anything, but then she said slowly, 'Maud, this is BIG!'"

I think Aunt Baby nailed it.

'BIG' says it all.

Each Tuskegee Airman could bring one guest to the inauguration. So, my father and mother planned to go to Washington, D.C.

My father forwarded e-mails from TAI with guidelines for attending the inauguration as well as press releases from the Presidential Inauguration Committee.

There was information about seating and where to show up. It was stressed that many of the roads would be closed off except to buses and authorized vehicles, so taking mass transit was strongly recommended. No backpacks were to be allowed past security check points. It was made clear that the weather would very likely be cold and anybody with health issues needed to think carefully about attending the event.

Early in December my mother had been bothered by sinus and

congestion problems, and a few weeks later she still wasn't feeling much better.

One morning my father called. "I've been talking to your mother. She's says that she doesn't want to fly to Washington, D.C. and then have to sit or stand outdoors in the cold for the ceremonies. Well, she has decided that she doesn't want to go on the trip after all."

"Oh, I see," I said, taking in this new development.

He continued, "I can take someone else instead… I was wondering if you or anyone else in your family would like to come with me."

This was the chance of a lifetime. I knew that. Other people would snap up this offer in a second. However, I have to admit that I hesitated, mainly because I know I don't do well standing around in the cold myself, since I have circulation issues. In any group I am usually the one with the coldest hands and feet. Even in moderate temperatures.

"Can I call you back?" I asked.

"Sure. Think about it."

I discussed this turn of events with Joe and Angela, my husband and fifteen-year-old daughter, since I was really conflicted. Yes, I wanted to go. And yes, I was worried about the cold.

"I'll go," Angela offered, "If you don't want to."

This was an offer from someone who never felt like wearing a jacket when it's cold. Of course she would go--the weather wouldn't affect her at all.

That got to me. No, this won't do, I thought to myself.

Aisha (19), Joe, Anita, and Angela Rowell (16), July, 2009

"No, no. That's OK. All right, then. I've decided. I'll go."

I called my dad back. I explained my initial reservation.

He listened, and then told me, "I know you can hack it."

I said to myself, "Wait, what's wrong with this conversation? Why is my father telling me I can hack it?"

"Sure," I told him. "I'll hack it."

"Great. I'm glad you're going with me."

What happened next is difficult to explain. With that decision, it felt as though – and this may not make a lot of sense – my entire center of gravity had shifted. Now, I would be one of those people who would witness this historic occasion. And thanks to the circumstances, I had been invited along with that group of select and distinguished gentlemen, the Original Tuskegee Airmen.

When tickets to the inauguration first became available after the November election, it was necessary to get them from a Congress person, or know somebody important who could get one for you. It would have been nice to know my Congresswoman, Lynn Woolsey, well enough for that, but I didn't know her at all. I just figured I didn't know anyone with connections. I was planning to watch the ceremony on TV along with millions of other people. So, then to suddenly have this opportunity was stunning. The irony was the fact that I had 'connections' all along, but wasn't aware of their existence. My connection to getting a ticket to the inauguration turned out to be my father. Who knew? It came out of the blue.

Now it was time to figure out the logistics of our road trip: Where to stay, and could we still get plane tickets to Washington, D.C.? Rooms in hotels were going for thousands of dollars, and many flights to D.C. were already booked. As my dad and I were discussing places to stay in D.C., it became clear that we'd have to find a family member or friend to put us up.

"Remember when we were in D.C. two years ago at the ceremonies for the Congressional Gold Medal, and cousin Alma Coggs Smith came to the reception that afternoon at the hotel?" I asked my father.

"Say, you're right. She surely was there," he recalled.

Alma was the daughter of my father's oldest brother Louis. She had lived in Chicago for many years, but was now in the D.C. area.

"You know, I'll give her a call," he said.

A couple of days after that, he called me back. "Good news. I spoke with Alma. Her place is too small, but she's arranged for us to stay with Marcy."

Marcy is Alma's daughter who lives with her family in Silver Spring, MD, right next to Washington, D.C. I hadn't seen Marcy for many years, so this would be the first time that I'd meet her husband Greg, and their children; Hannah, 14; Alston, 12; John,10; and Caleb, 8 years old.

"That's great!" I replied. I was relieved and grateful for the way things were working out, and I was glad we'd be staying with family while we were in the D.C. area.

As we were preparing for our trip, my father received information from TAI about the seating arrangements at the Inauguration.

"The Tuskegee Airmen will be seated near the front of the stage for the ceremonies." My father told me. This was wonderful and such a great honor.

Then there was an update. "The Tuskegee Airmen are going to be seated on the stage, with their guests nearby. I can hardly believe it!" This was even more wonderful and fantastic.

Even though all that was exciting enough, the next thing we found out was that the "Good Morning America" show on ABC was going to do a piece on the Tuskegee Airmen and the Inauguration, which would air on the morning of the Inauguration. Co-anchor Robin Roberts, whose own father, Lawrence Roberts, had been a Tuskegee Airman, would conduct the interview. "This is incredible," my father said when he called. In my mind, I could easily see him shaking his head in disbelief, probably thinking, "I never could have imagined …all this."

Certainly, "all this" was the overarching sentiment for this extraordinary and historic experience.

The recognition and appreciation for exemplary service, accolades long overdue, and being able to see this day come to pass in his lifetime.

The "Good Morning America" piece would consist of Robin Roberts talking to three Tuskegee Airmen.

Then the phone rang. It was my mother.

"Your father can hardly contain himself. I don't know what we're going to do with him. I believe he's floating right now."

Why?

He had been selected as one of three Tuskegee Airmen who would participate in the interview!

Appearing on national TV at the time of the Presidential Inauguration--amazing! Could it get any better than this? Going to D.C. was evolving into a multi-faceted and astonishing trip.

My father grabbed the phone to tell me that another Tuskegee Airman from San Antonio was going to D.C. also, and would participate in the "GMA" interview.

" 'Mule' Miles is coming to the inauguration too," he said.

" 'Mule' Miles?" I repeated. "His name is 'Mule'?"

"Well, that's the name he's known by. You know, he was one of the best players in the Negro Baseball League," he explained.

"Really! So what is Mule's actual given name?"

"His name is John, but lots of folks still call him 'Mule'".

"And how did he get the name Mule?" I asked.

"The story was that he was such a powerful batter, his coach commented 'He hits the ball as hard as a mule kicks.'"

My father had met 'Mule' Miles in the San Antonio chapter of TAI.

It turned out that Mr. Miles and my father were featured in a front page story of the San Antonio Express News about their upcoming trip to D.C.

I began to notice a recurring visceral reaction when I would tell someone about the trip to Washington. Just mentioning that we were going was enough excitement for most people. Then finding out about the seating, and the GMA interview, it was almost too much to take in at once. Two of my friends said exactly the same thing after I told them all the news. "You're giving me goose bumps!"

When we were on a stopover at the Burbank airport on our way to D.C., two flight attendants had the same response after they asked us where we were going. The interesting thing was that we spoke to them individually in different parts of the plane, yet they each said the same thing. "I'm getting chills!"

The anticipation and the hope surrounding Barack Obama's inauguration was immense, and the significance of participating in and witnessing the event was so great, that our trip was destined to become the shining jewel in our family archives.

There was a news release from the JCCIC (Joint Congressional Committee on Inaugural Ceremonies) regarding important considerations for travel in the Capitol.

"The weather in Washington in January is usually quite cold and often rainy or snowy. Please think carefully about whether you can stand outside in cold weather in a large crowd for up to six hours, and whether you are ready for long delays getting home afterwards..."

Joe and his family had lived in Washington, D.C. for a few years, and he told me the same thing; "It's going to be cold."

From prior ski trips to Lake Tahoe, I already had warm gloves, leggings, thick socks, turtleneck sweaters, hats and scarves. I decided I needed thermal underwear too. I went to Santa Rosa Ski and Sport, and ended up buying what the package referred to as "Warmwear – Base Layer Tops and Bottoms" for extra body warmth. I bought some black faux-Ugg snow boots at Target, and along with a heavy winter coat, it looked like I had all the clothing I needed for the trip.

I knew that I should pack a couple of handkerchiefs as well. That was because when Joe, Angela and I were sitting on the couch in the family room, watching on TV as Barack Obama became elected President, I had become emotional. At first, I just dabbed my eyes and nose with a couple of tissues, but then it became necessary to hold the box of Kleenex in my lap as I wiped the tears from my eyes and blew my nose.

I found two handkerchiefs in Joe's dresser drawer. They were of nice, crisp, white linen, embossed with the letter "R" in the upper-right hand corner. He had received a package of them as a Christmas present a few years ago, and they had never been used.

'Perfect,' I thought. 'I'll need these.'

I made sure to pack into my carry-on bag the book, "8 Simple Rules to Live By," written by Robin Roberts. My father had read her preceding book, "7 Simple Rules to Live By," and had recommended it to me since he was impressed with her straightforward, easy-to-read writing style. He had pointed out that when she spoke to groups, she didn't use prepared material, but just spoke "from the heart." Since my father spoke to groups often, he thought that was a great technique.

I not only read his copy, but when "8 Simple Rules to Live By," came out, we both bought a copy. It included a lot about her experience with overcoming breast cancer. My father found that topic particularly interesting, since as a radiologist, his specialty was breast disease and breast cancer diagnosis, and he had overcome prostate cancer himself.

I decided I would bring my copy of her book with me to the "Good Morning America" interview and ask her to sign it.

Now, it seemed that I had included everything I needed to take with me.

We left Oakland on Saturday, January 17th on Southwest flight #1935. The flight didn't require us to change planes, but we made stops in Burbank, Las Vegas, and Chicago on our way to Washington, D.C.

The weather was perfect. At both Burbank and Las Vegas, the temperature was in the low 70's. The scenery below was crisp and clear as we flew over the country in the bright, blue sky. We figured it was nice to enjoy it now, because the flight attendant informed us that the temperature at Midway Airport in Chicago was 20 degrees –cold.

On the leg from Burbank to Las Vegas, we were still seated in row 15, which is where my father preferred sitting, since he felt it was safer to be over the wing. A nice friendly gentleman sat next to me on the aisle seat. He said he was going on to Albuquerque, then to Colorado for a ski trip. We got to talking about aviation, and he mentioned that his great-uncle was the first pilot to make an authorized flight over the Golden Gate Bridge. I told him my father was a Tuskegee Airman, and it turned out my seat mate knew a lot about the Tuskegee Airmen. He was impressed and wanted to shake hands with my dad. After he shook his hand, he was very excited.

"I've shaken hands with Bill Clinton and thought that was something, but now that I've shaken hands with your father--that's really special!" he said to me.

The way he looked at his hand, almost with a sense of amazement, it seemed to me he could have been thinking, "I don't think I'm going to be washing my hands for a while." There it was again; the association by handshake--a special connection. To be sure, whenever he is identified as a Tuskegee Airman, traveling with my dad was like being on the road with a rock star.

While we were on the ground in Las Vegas, we talked to two of the flight attendants for a while. We introduced ourselves and found out that their names were Tara and Sabrina.

As we were chatting, Tara informed us, "Bette Midler was on the plane when we flew from Burbank to Las Vegas."

"Really!" I said.

"Is that right?" my father asked.

"Yes, we see quite a few celebrities. It's convenient for them to fly from Burbank to Las Vegas if they're doing a show there," she continued. "She was sitting in row 11."

Neither my father nor I had noticed her there. If we'd been paying attention and looked toward the front of the plane as the other passengers boarded in Burbank, we might have recognized her as she was taking her seat.

Bette Midler had been sitting four rows up from us!

A light dusting of snow was falling and it was approximately 20 degrees outside as our plane pulled up to the gate at Midway Airport in Chicago.

Apparently, the flight attendants had informed the captain that my father was a Tuskegee Airman, and he wanted to meet him. He invited us up to the front and introduced himself as Sean Howard. After he and my dad had talked for a bit, he was very gracious and asked my father if he'd like to see the cockpit of the airplane.

"Sure!" my dad replied.

So Captain Howard let my dad come in, look around and sit in the captain's seat, while he stepped just outside the cockpit.

"This is fantastic!" my father said as he looked around at all the instruments, gauges, mechanical equipment and myriad panels with various colors of lights that were in the front, on the sides, and overhead in the cockpit.

"I guess things look a whole lot different than when you flew," Captain Howard said as he saw my dad checking out all the electronic devices surrounding him.

"Absolutely," my dad replied emphatically.

Sean Howard came back inside and sat in the copilot's chair. Then a flight attendant took a picture with my dad's iPhone of the two of them sitting

Granville and Anita in the cockpit

together in the cockpit. It was a great shot.

I was watching my father take in all the sights of the cockpit, when Captain Howard asked me if I'd like to come in the cockpit and check it out too.

Carpe diem.

"Yes!" I said.

Captain Howard came out, and I went over and sat in the copilot's chair.

So there we were, with me riding shotgun in the cockpit of Flight #1935!

Captain Howard got a wonderful snapshot of both of us sitting up there and smiling in the cockpit.

That picture, my father said later, is his favorite shot of the two of us together. It's a classic.

It's hard to describe the thoughts I had as I looked in front of me.

On one hand there was the notion of, 'If I knew what I was doing, I could take off and fly this thing.' An ineffable, although fleeting, sense of empowerment.

However, on the other hand, I had a silent, heartfelt prayer in my mind; 'Oh please, dear Lord, don't let me touch the wrong button and break something up in here.'

Since we had to wait at Midway longer than expected while the wings of the plane were being de-iced, I decided I would go into the terminal to walk around and stretch my legs. I had done the same thing during our stopover at the Las Vegas Airport.

I walked up to the front of the plane, and asked the copilot, "How much time is there until the plane starts boarding again?"

"About thirty minutes," he replied.

"So, I'll be back in twenty minutes then," I said.

"If you're not back, we'll hold the plane for you," he assured me.

I knew he had said that lightly, but his statement caught me off guard. No one had ever told me they would hold a plane for me.

"Oh, that won't be a problem. I'll be back soon," I told him.

It was freezing cold as I walked up the corridor to the terminal, thinking, 'In real life, no copilot would say that to me.'

Which made me consider; 'So, what does that make this--my unreal life?'

After I returned and other passengers boarded, the mood of the entire plane revved up. Many people were in high spirits. Clearly, there were lots of Obama supporters, who were understandably excited since Chicago was his home town, and they were on their way to the Capitol for his inauguration. It was an airborne good time on a Saturday night.

At this point, I should mention that Southwest Airlines is very supportive of the Tuskegee Airmen and actively honors and respects their accomplishments.

In fact, on the side of one of their airplanes, there is a large image, in color, of the profile of a Tuskegee Airman in his WWII flight gear.

One time when I was at the Southwest Airlines terminal in the San Antonio Airport, I saw this plane on the tarmac and was impressed with the artistry.

And since I'm writing about Southwest Airlines, I have to describe what happened when my parents and I were in Washington, D.C. in March, 2007 to attend the ceremonies at the Capitol when the Tuskegee Airmen received the Congressional Gold Medal.

Many of the Airmen had been contacted by Senators and/or members of Congress from the states or districts where they lived, or where they were raised, to come by and meet them while they were in D.C.

So, my father and anyone in his party were invited to three meetings.

First, we were invited to have breakfast with Congressman Charles Gonzalez from San Antonio, Texas, in the Members' Dining Hall in the Capitol, on the day before the ceremony.

Second, we were invited to meet with Senator Blanche Lincoln from Arkansas that afternoon in her office; both my parents were born and raised in Arkansas. Also, she was familiar with my father, since she gave a speech right after my father was inducted into the Arkansas Black Hall of Fame in 2001.

And third, the morning of the ceremony, we met with Senator Kay Bailey Hutchison for coffee at her office.

As each invitation was extended, we were awestruck and looked forward to these meetings.

We had enjoyed meeting and visiting with Congressman Gonzalez, and as we were on our way out of the Dining Hall, a tall, imposing man was walked in.

My dad and this man looked at each other, grinned and laughed, and then slapped each other on the back.

He greeted my father, "Gran!"

"Hey, Herb!" my dad replied.

They chuckled at some inside joke having to do with the last time they had seen each other.

My mother and I exchanged quick glances; she was probably wondering the same things I was:

"Who is this guy?" and

"Who would ever expect to run into someone they know in the Members' Dining Hall in the Capitol?"

My father introduced us to Herb Kelleher.

As I recall, it seemed that Congressman Gonzalez and Mr. Kelleher already knew each other.

After they chatted briefly, we were on our way.

Congressman Gonzalez was very kind and gracious with his time, and took us to the steps of the Capitol for a photo-op with their official photographer.

After he left us, we asked my dad about Herb Kelleher.

"Herb Kelleher," he explained, "is Chairman of the Board of Southwest Airlines."

"Oh, really!" we said.

"And you know him…how?" I asked.

"We met back in 2003. There was an Air Centennial Celebration at Brook Air Force Base, sponsored by the San Antonio Academy, a prep school in San Antonio. We were on an aviation panel together, along with Chuck Yeager…the first pilot to break the sound barrier," he replied.

"Now that you mention it, I do remember the newspaper article you sent with a picture of the three of you at the event," I said.

"Yes. That's when it was."

That's when I thought, 'Small world…isn't it?'

We arrived at Dulles Airport where Marcy's husband Greg met us. We drove to their home in Silver Spring, Maryland, which is just across the border from the District of Columbia. We arrived late at night. Marcy was up to meet us, but the children were sleeping. We would meet them in the morning.

Sunday, January 18, 2009

On Sunday morning we met all four of the children for the first time; Hannah, Alston, John and Caleb. I was glad to be staying with family. We enjoyed their warmth and kind hospitality all throughout our stay. My father and I, Greg, and all four of the children took the Metro to the L'Enfant Plaza station and made our way to the Smithsonian National Air and Space Museum. At the Smithsonian, we were directed to the WWII Aviators Section, where the "Good Morning America" interview was to take place.

When we got there we met the producer, Karen Leo, and watched the crew as they set up for the interview. Marcy's mother Alma joined us there. We looked around at some of the exhibits and memorabilia and admired the colorful mural on the back wall depicting WWII planes, pilots, and events.

While we waited, we talked to the three other Tuskegee Airmen. Firs we visited with John 'Mule' Miles from San Antonio, Texas.

Then, we were introduced to Dabney Montgomery from New York City. He had an interesting life story. He has been a civil rights activist, a bodyguard for Martin Luther King, Jr., a chaplain, a ballet dancer, a social services worker, a community board member and historian. He lives in Harlem, N.Y.

Also there was Merrill Ross from Topeka, Kansas, along with his wife Barbara, their son Brian and his wife Kim from Maryland. Mr. Ross had been the principal of an elementary school and the coach of a high school basketball team in Topeka.

At age 89, Merrill Ross was the second oldest Tuskegee Airman. We were told that a man named Clarence C. Jamison, at age 91, was the oldest Tuskegee Airman.

We also met Jennifer Myers, who is with Tuskegee Airmen, Inc., and was instrumental in organizing the "GMA" interview.

I gave my camera to Hannah. I had seen pictures she had taken and they were very good. I realized that a nimble fourteen-year-old girl would be able to get into tight spaces, crawl around, and take pictures from more angle than an older person such as myself. She was quite resourceful, and moved around the crew's equipment and people on the set quietly and unobtrusively.

My father said to Hannah, "Please make sure to get a shot of me when I shake Robin Robert's hand for the first time."

So there it was again--the association conferred by a handshake.

I got Robin's book and a pen out of my tote bag and put them where they would be handy.

There was a momentary hush when Robin Roberts entered the room. She had such a commanding presence, and I found her to be strikingly tall and beautiful in person. I figured she could be around 5'10", and with 2" heels on, she was nearly 6' tall. She seemed taller and thinner to me than she appeared on TV. (Many in our family group said the same thing afterward, and Hannah reminded us that the camera adds 10 lbs.)

As she was introduced to the Tuskegee Airmen, my father shook her hand. Hannah got the shot.

They spoke of the historical significance of the Tuskegee Airmen as being the "wingmen" whose endeavors helped pave the way to a time when an African-American would be elected President of the United States--a time that they all never imagined they would live to see. They talked about how Barack Obama said that he felt he was standing on the shoulders of the Tuskegee Airmen.

She interviewed John 'Mule' Miles, Dabney Montgomery, and my father. Their responses were heartfelt and emotional.

Here are some of the Q & A's from the interview that was included in the broadcast:

RR: What does it feel like to be here in Washington, D.C., at the invitation…You were invited by the President!
JM: It's a great honor to me. I never expected to see an African-American elected President in my lifetime. This is wonderful to me, and I'm here to shake hands with Obama and hug Michelle.(smile)
DM: (in a deep resonant voice)When you asked me that question a few seconds ago, a tear came out of this eye, because I always looked forward to this event coming to pass for the next generation,and here I am looking at it and taking part in it. What a feeling! Tremendous feeling!
GC: One word: Unimaginable! And that says it!
RR: What piece of advice would you want to give Barack Obama?
GC: Just keep on doing what he's doing, that's what I would say. "Keep on doing what you're doing."
DB: "Remain calm. He's the coolest cat I've ever seen!"

(He chuckled--the rest smiled and nodded their heads in agreement.)

JM: "You have a good mind, a bright mind, and I like your attitude--it's wonderful. Continue what you're doing, and may God bless you."

Granville Coggs, Dabney Coleman, Robin Roberts, and John 'Mule' Miles

After the interview wrapped up, Robin graciously took the time to have pictures taken with the Airmen and many of their family members, and signed the copy of her book that I had brought. Before we left the WWII Aviator's Section, she kissed each of the Tuskegee Airmen on the cheek, and it seemed to me that each one began to melt away for just a moment.

Then the "GMA" crew wanted to go over to the African-American Aviation Section to get some shots of the Tuskegee Airmen, and filmed them as they walked down the corridor. As soon as people noticed the lights and cameras, they saw Robin Roberts and then recognized the Tuskegee Airmen, who wore their blue caps with "Tuskegee Airmen" on them. A crowd began to form quickly. When they got to the African-American Aviation Section, and it was officially announced who these men were, there was a great round of cheering and clapping, and the glow of camera flashes going off.

The "GMA" crew kept shooting as the Airmen looked at the historic memorabilia surrounding them. The Airmen were lingering near the front of the room when they came upon the Congressional Gold Medal that they had been awarded in 2007, which was in a glass case on top of a pedestal. The gold was shining brightly.

When I saw it, I remember thinking, 'Ah, so here it is! The actual Congressional Gold Medal'.

At the 2007 ceremonies at the Capitol it was mentioned that the actual Congressional Gold Medal, made of solid gold, would be on display at the Smithsonian. Each of the Original Tuskegee Airmen was presented with beautiful and striking bronze replica that day.

The cameramen were getting shots of the Tuskegee Airmen as they visited with admirers, signed autographs, and posed for pictures with people. I stood by the pedestal next to Robin Roberts.

As we watched the crowd surround them, we talked about how emotional it was to see these special men so honored and respected. We also talked about how, as daughters of Original Tuskegee Airmen, we were so proud of our fathers and their accomplishments.

Gazing at the three of them, I said, "Doesn't all this just go right to your heart?"

"It sure does," she agreed.

I noticed that when we mentioned how this went right to our hearts, we both put our right hand over our heart, at the same time.

John 'Mule' Miles, Dabney Coleman, Merrill Ross, Robin Roberts, Jennifer Myers, and Granville Coggs

Monday, January 19, 2009

My dad's iPhone rang at 8:30 a.m. Monday morning and it was Jennifer Myers on the line.

I took the call. She wanted to find out if my dad would be able to do an interview this afternoon with a reporter from Montgomery, Alabama who was doing a segment on the Tuskegee Airmen. Of course, my father said "Yes!", and she said that he should meet with reporter Kim Hendrix at 12:15 p.m. to prepare for their live broadcast at 12:30 p.m. She told him to come to the intersection of 7th Avenue and Madison Drive at the Capitol Mall, where many of the media trucks, vans, trailers, and satellite dishes, etc. were located, and to look for a truck with WBTV-News on the side.

Talk about "out of the blue!" What a way to start the day.

So, we told Marcy and her family, and we all hurried to get ready to leave. With the exception of Greg, who was at work, all of us took the Metro down to the Capitol, just as we had done the day before.

As we walked through the media area to meet Kim Hendrix, we passed by the platform where MSNBC was broadcasting live, where I could make out the back of Soledad O'Brien, in front of a crowd of people assembled there. I knew that was her because earlier that morning, the TV channel at the house was on MSNBC, and they had shown her talking to a group of people from the very platform in front of us.

A bustling throng filled the Capitol Mall and we could hear the sounds of the concert blaring from the steps of the Capitol. We were too far away though to make out who was singing or what was being said.

I must not have made the detail about the truck clear to my father, because when we got to the corner of 7th and Madison and could see lots of TV trucks lined up, he stopped and didn't walk any further.

"Dad," I said, "We've got to keep going. We're not there yet."

He didn't move.

"She said the corner of 7th and Madison, so I'm staying right here," he said.

"Yes, come to the corner of 7th and Madison and look for the truck with WBTV-News on the side," I replied.

"I think I should stay here."

He, apparently, was under the impression that someone would meet us on the corner, and wasn't about to budge from that spot.

By this time, it was about 12:05; Marcy and I had looked up the block and could see the truck with WBTV-News in bold letters on the side.

Marcy came over to assure him, "Uncle Granville, we really need to go to that truck up there," and both of us pointed up the block.

We soon convinced him, and he said, "OK. All right, then."

When we reached the WBTV-News truck, I went up and knocked on the side door. A man opened the door.

"Hi," I said. "We're looking for the reporter Kim Hendrix. My father is supposed to meet her here at 12:15 for an interview."

"What's her name again?" he asked.

"Kim Hendrix," I repeated.

"I don't know her," he said.

"You see, there's more than one station working out of this truck," he explained.

"Hold on," he told us. "Let me go ask someone else."

After he turned around, we turned to each other with that look. The look that asks: "What the heck?"

He spoke to another man in the truck, to see if he knew her. The man said something to him. Then he faced us again and asked, "Is she a blonde?"

We had no idea what she looked like.

"I don't know," I answered.

What I did know, is that it was about time to be meeting with her, and I was becoming more and more anxious.

I glanced at my watch, while he conferred with his co-worker again.

"We think she must be the blonde. She's right over there," he said and pointed towards a spot on the grass by a tree not far away.

"OK, thanks," I replied, and we headed over to where he had pointed.

I went up to her and said, "We're looking for Kim Hendrix. I'm with my father Dr. Coggs here, and he has an interview with her.

"Why, yes, that's me," she told us.

After introductions, she explained that she was with WFSA-12 News, which is the CBS affiliate in Montgomery.

WFSA-12 News broadcasts to the southern and central regions of Alabama, and covers the area where Tuskegee is located. To give me a historical perspective, my dad informed me that in the 1950's and 1960's, WFSA-12 News had provided extensive coverage of the Civil Rights marches, protests, and activism during the turbulent times of the Civil Rights Movement in the South.

As they became acquainted, my dad and Kim discovered that they had a lot in common as Texans; my parents had been living in Texas for over thirty years in San Antonio, and Kim is a Texas native.

During the interview she asked him questions about his thoughts and impressions as a Tuskegee Airman regarding Barack Obama's Inauguration, his views of the event from his own historical experiences, and other related topics.

At one point, she asked my father what his daughters thought about his presence at the Inauguration, and he pointed to me and said, "Well here's the oldest. You can ask her."

It took probably all of one second for the following thoughts to race through my head:

"No, he didn't!"

"He knows this is live TV right?"

"He does not know that right before this, Hannah had informed me that my nose was turning red, and I had explained that it does that when the weather is really cold."

"Kim Hendrix is all camera-ready, whereas I am definitely not!"

"I could use some make-up over here!"

"I've got to think of something coherent to say, real quickly."

My mind focused on key words/sound bites:"Proud;""Excited;" "Privileged."

Anita, Granville, Kim Hendrix, and Andre Morgan

At this point the camera panned over to where I was standing. As I recollect, I came up with three sentences, each featuring one of my key words. Then there was another question or two.

After the interview, we met her camera-man, Andre Morgan, who was from Bessemer, Alabama. We posed for pictures that were taken with my camera and my father's iPhone.

As we wrapped up our session, Jennifer Myers showed up. She had gotten a call from a radio talk-show in Sydney, Australia. They wanted to do a live interview with a Tuskegee Airman, and she asked my father if he would do it. Of course, my dad said "Yes!", and she told him that talk show host Ollie Benson would be calling at 2:30 p.m. this afternoon.

We gave Marcy's home phone number to Jennifer so that the radio show could call him on a land line, and began walking toward the Metro to head back to Silver Spring, Maryland.

As we made our way through the crowds and vendors selling all sorts of 'Obamabilia,' Marcy and Jennifer were remarking that they had never seen so many African Americans in downtown Washington, D.C. before.

Jennifer said it seemed to her that black people in D.C. felt that the Capitol was "Ours" now.

I called that yet another example of 'The Obama Effect'.

We got back to Marcy's house, and around 2:30 p.m. my father took the call from Sydney, Australia, and did another live interview.

After the phone interview, my dad and I talked about how the day had unfolded and how astonishing and exciting it had been. He was sitting there thinking about it; shaking his head a bit, as if in disbelief.

"Unimaginable."

The Big Day
Tuesday, January 20, 2009

We were up very early, and Alma picked us up at 5:30 a.m. to take us to Bolling Air Force Base. As we drove away, we saw crowds of people streaming down the sidewalks in the pre-dawn darkness to get to the Metro. She dropped us off at 6:00 a.m. and we made our way to the Dining Hall in the Officer's Club. It was a huge, spacious room with high ceilings adorned with crystal chandeliers. White linen tablecloths covered clusters of tables. There was a breakfast buffet with scrambled eggs, bacon, sausage, grits, toast, biscuits, gravy, cranberry juice, orange juice, coffee, tea…the works.

My dad greeted a couple of Airmen who were near our table. One of them was Milton Crenshaw. My father told me that he was a venerable flight instructor at Tuskegee. I was struck by his bearing, as he stood very straight and tall. My dad confided later that he too was impressed with Mr. Crenshaw since, "He looks better than I do, and he has to be around ninety years old." The other was Lorenzo Holloway, a fellow Airman from Detroit, Michigan.

At 7:00 a.m. we were directed to walk down a long corridor to reach the next room. There we received our packet that contained an official Inaugural Invitation and Inaugural Program, both beautiful and elegant with gold lettering embossed on a heavy weight vellum paper. We were also given a ticket - the much coveted Inaugural ticket - that admitted us to Section 15 at the West Front of the Capitol, where a special area had been reserved to seat the approximately two hundred and twenty-five Tuskegee Airmen and their guests.

Next, we all went through security checks. After my dad and I had gone through the metal detector and been "wanded", I looked over to my right and noticed a gentleman who resembled Earl Graves, Jr. the publisher of Black Enterprise magazine. At the beginning of each issue there is a section, 'Publisher's Page", with a picture of Earl Graves, Jr. along with his column discussing pertinent topics. I asked my father if that could be him, and he replied that he thought so. He decided he'd go over and ask—it was he.

There were ten buses waiting outside, and we were seated on bus #5. After we were settled, each of us received a warm, red, fleece blanket to use during the inauguration.

We were told to return to the same bus after the ceremonies to get a box lunch. We were also given packets of hand warmers which worked pretty well.

As our caravan neared the Capitol, it was striking to see so many people walking towards the inauguration area and already lined up to go inside the sections designated for ticket holders. The buses parked close to the Capitol, so that essentially the only thing we needed to do was walk across Constitution Avenue, make our way to a security checkpoint and enter the correct gate section. We found our seats reserved for the Tuskegee Airmen and their guests.

It was so cold outside! We were bundled up in layers of clothes; sweaters, heavy coats, hats, gloves and scarves. Still we felt the freezing, biting cold permeate our bodies. I was told that the temperature was in the low 20's, and with the wind chill factor it was around 17 degrees.

As I walked toward the Capitol, the important and historical significance of this day welled up inside me especially since I was surrounded by this distinguished group of African-American men. These men, who had served their country in WWII and established an impeccable record, were here at the invitation of Barack Obama to witness the swearing in of our nation's first African-American President. As I write these words, I get teary all over again and feel goose bumps. What an honor and privilege to participate in this presidential inauguration. I was so proud of my father and so proud of all these Original Tuskegee Airmen. I knew that I was extremely fortunate and profoundly blessed to have the opportunity to experience this trip of a lifetime.

Most of the events today have been covered by the media, so I won't go into great detail. I just want to convey my most vivid impressions.

The sun came out, the day was clear, and the sky was blue - that's about as good as it gets in Washington, D.C. in January. It seemed that the sun was at its brightest when the ceremonies began. As we took our seats we faced the Capitol, but then when we turned around, it was so stunning, so astonishing, to see the sea of people before us, reaching all the way to the Washington Monument. I had never in my life seen anything like that; an amazing number of people, many holding flags that rippled like waves throughout the crowd. There was an electricity of anticipation and brightness that flowed throughout the air.

It seemed incredible that the two men who came and sat next to us were no other than Lee Archer and Earl Graves, Jr. Lee Archer, of course, was the ace fighter pilot of the Tuskegee Airmen, whose exploits in WWII are legendary. He sat right next to my dad, with Earl Graves, Jr. to his left.

I watched to see if my father was going to say "Hello" and introduce himself (us) to Mr. Archer. As we waited for the event to begin, there were people who came over after they recognized him, and wanted to shake his hand or pose for a snapshot with him. My dad didn't speak with him though. He must have decided that since this day was so special and momentous, he was not going to bother Lee Archer so that he could fully soak in the experience.

From time to time however, I would look to my left without turning my head, as subtly and covertly as I could, to glance quickly at Mr. Archer. And I was struck by three things. First, his eyes--seemed so keen and thoughtful. Then there was his youthful demeanor. If I didn't know better, I would have guessed he was in his sixties. Later my father remarked, "He looks better than I do, and he must be eighty-nine years old." I thought he was handsome.

As the ceremonies began, a procession of dignitaries came to the front of the stage and took their seats. Everyone, of course, was waiting to see when Barack Obama would come out of the Capitol building. Then, at the very first glimpse of him, the crowd roared, I got all choked up with a lump in my throat, and tears came to my eyes. I could see that it was already time to reach in my coat pocket and pull out my handkerchief. I had decided to bring two handkerchiefs with me that morning; one for my pocket, and one stashed in my tote bag for backup. While I was sitting there, I was dabbing my eyes and nose with the handkerchief quite often. I knew that if I was at home on the sofa in front of the TV, I would probably have broken down in tears. I looked around cautiously to see if anyone else was overcome with emotion. However, this was a stoic group surrounding me in my seating area--men trained as fighter pilots. I knew that it would just not do to start sobbing uncontrollably in the midst of these people and their guests.
I'd just have to contain myself.

My first thoughts after I saw Barack Obama were: 'They let him come!'

I guess I was thinking of 'they' as in those who would do him harm, or prevent him from showing up.

'He's here. He's OK. He made it. This is really it. Oh, my God.'

Immediately after Supreme Court Justice John Roberts had sworn in Barack Obama, there was a huge roar from the crowd, along with cheering and lots of applause. After Obama said, "So help me, God," cannons boomed,

Granville and Anita

and the sound filled the air, echoing like thunder throughout the Capitol Mall.

After the ceremonies, the big-screen Jumbotrons showed the other side of the Capitol, where we could see George and Laura Bush preparing to leave Washington and walking toward an awaiting helicopter. They waved and climbed in. As the rotors began to whirl, we could hear the sound. After the helicopter lifted off, we could see it rising above the Capitol. Its noise became louder and louder as it banked our way. That's when the crowd began cheering and shouting. One group of people spontaneously started to sing and chant the chorus of the song by Steam, that goes "Nah, nah, nah, nah –

nah, nah, nah, nah – hey, hey, hey - goodbye". Pretty soon, more and more people joined in and repeated the chorus a few more times. When the word "Goodbye" came at the end of the chorus, the crowd shouted it out loudly and emphatically each time. Many waved at the helicopter as it flew away.

As my father and I left our seats and moved into the aisle, an Airman who was behind us came up beside me. He nodded toward Lee Archer and asked me, "You do know who that is, don't you?"

For a second I was thinking, 'What is this, a trick question or something? Wouldn't everyone here know Lee Archer if they saw him?'

I answered, "That's Lee Archer."

"That's right," he said, and then joined the others going up the aisle. I figured he was just checking to make sure I knew who was who, and what was what.

As we made our way back to the gate, there were so many people, so closely packed together going in the same direction, I felt as though if I put my elbows out to the side, I would be lifted up off my feet and carried along with the crowd as it was moving.

While people were filing out en masse, it was wonderful to see how the crowd, estimated to be almost two million people, was so well-behaved and civilized. Everyone seemed respectful, joyful, and excited to be a part of American history.

We walked to the buses and discovered that our caravan wouldn't be heading back to Bolling Air Force Base right away as planned. During the ceremonies, Constitution Avenue had been blocked off with barricades in preparation for the Inaugural Parade, and the buses couldn't drive out to the street. So, even though I hadn't expected to see the parade, I was excited to have the chance to watch. Seeing a Presidential motorcade go by was the opportunity of a lifetime, and even better, it was Barack Obama in the Presidential State Car.

After we got back to the bus, the driver handed out box lunches. I took one that had a turkey and cheddar cheese on wheat sandwich, an apple, a bag of BBQ chips, and a chocolate chip cookie. I will never forget this box lunch--simply because it was the box lunch that I ate on the day of the Presidential Inauguration.

Our bus was parked close to Constitution Avenue. After lunch, I got off with a few other people, walked over to the sidewalk and stood behind the barricades. We were hoping to get a glimpse of the start of the parade. The sidewalk was full and the crowd was two or three people deep.

It was so cold outside, and many of these people had been standing there for hours! I knew they had to be chilled to the bone. The parade was delayed forty-five minutes to an hour from its original starting time. At one point we heard the sirens of an ambulance headed toward the Capitol. Later on in the day, we found out that Senator Ted Kennedy had suffered a seizure at the Inaugural Luncheon.

I was talking to a man next to me who lived in D.C., and he explained how you could tell which car was the Presidential vehicle in the motorcade.

"You look for the one where the cars in front and the cars in back have armed secret service men hanging on and standing on the sideboards."

However, when the parade started, we had to get back on the bus, since all the drivers wanted to get out as quickly as possible at the end of the parade. They didn't want to round up people who were outside dispersed in the crowd. So, we watched from inside the bus. And since it was parked only about fifteen yards or so from the street, we could see just about everything.

There were honor guards and marching bands at the beginning of the parade. Then they were followed by many other groups and organizations, with lots of pomp and circumstance.

Finally we could see rows of policemen on motorcycles and the procession of police cars with their lights flashing preceding the presidential motorcade.

The Cadillac Presidential Limousine was guarded by four Secret Service agents, one at each corner of the state car, who walked alongside it as it made its way down the street. The Secret Service agents were 'Men in Black,' who wore black overcoats, black pants, black shoes, and had on white shirts with colorful ties. The car had two small flags on the front of the hood on each side. One was the American flag, the other, the Presidential flag. (The Presidential flag has the presidential coat of arms--an eagle surrounded by fifty stars, holding an olive branch in one talon, and arrows in the other against a blue background.)

Behind this car was a row of three vehicles, two more black Cadillac limousines and a black SUV. The SUV had four Secret Service agents standing on its running boards; two were facing forward, and the other two were facing the rear and to the side of the vehicle. The back of the SUV was open, where agents with guns scanned the crowd.

The sight of the motorcade was both impressive and exciting. As the Presidential State Car went by, a man behind me exclaimed, "I think I see him. That's Obama. I can tell by his ears!"

I smiled when he said that because I wasn't able to make out anything inside the car as it drove by since the windows were so heavily tinted. It was just cool that I saw the car that held Barack Obama.

After the parade was over we headed for Bolling Air Force Base. Every bus in the caravan had a sign on each side that said, "The Tuskegee

Airmen," so as we made our way through the city streets of D.C., at times there was waving, clapping, and shouting from groups of people as they recognized the Tuskegee Airmen.

Marcy picked us up at the Air Force Base accompanied by my cousin Anne Coggs Smith, who had come to D.C. from Chicago for the inauguration. Anne is Alma's older sister. We went back to Marcy's house, where we all had to change quickly into our formal evening outfits since our cousin, Pam Coggs Alexander, had organized an Inaugural Gala Celebration, with my father as a special guest. The Gala started at 7:00 p.m. and we were running late because we had stayed at the Capitol and watched the parade. The Celebration was at Gallaudet University in northeast Washington, D.C.

When Marcy, Anne, my dad and I got there, the evening was getting into full swing. There was a live band performing and dinner was served with a champagne toast. At the front of the room was a huge screen which showed the live coverage of Barack and Michelle Obama dancing and mingling as they went from Gala to Gala.

After dinner, the toastmaster was our cousin Spencer Coggs, who is a state senator from Wisconsin. Following Spencer was Cuba Gooding, Sr. He sang some songs from his new CD, but when he started talking, I said to Marcy, "He sounds just like Cuba Gooding, Jr." Then after a moment we both said, "No, Cuba Gooding, Jr. sounds just like his father."

After that, the 'Prezidential D.J.s' got people up out of their seats and onto the dance floor. There was a photographer at the back of the hall where a full-size cut-out of Barack Obama in a dark suit was the perfect prop for people who wanted their pictures taken in groups or by themselves. The shots made it look like Barack Obama was standing by you or shaking your hand.

Before we left to go to Washington D.C. and up until today, my father was hoping to get the chance to shake Barack Obama's hand. I had told him, "Yeah, you, and a million other people in D.C." And yet, he was undaunted.

So it seemed perfect when I came upon him along with Spencer and his wife, Gershia, posing for a shot together with what I called the "Faux-Bama." It looked like my dad was shaking Obama's hand. He loved the shot and had the photographer make a print and put it in a matte frame.

By the end of the evening, I was getting really tired. We'd been up since 3:30 a.m., had a big day, and a long day. My feet were killing me since I'd been wearing heels all night, and it was time to wrap things up.

Later that night, as we talked about the events packed into this one single day, my dad said, "I would never have thought that I'd see this day, and be a part of it.

"That was really something," I replied. "What a day."

"I am sooo glad you invited me to come along," I said.

"My pleasure," he replied.

I've heard others who were present at the inauguration describe it as a "transformational" experience. It definitely was, and even more than that for me. It was an opportunity that fell into my lap by serendipity--as the guest of a Tuskegee Airman—it gave me a special and unique perspective. I appreciate how fortunate I was and know it's not likely to happen again. The energy of that day reminded me what it means to be a proud daughter and a hopeful human being.

I will always remember the electricity of those two million people and the roar a crowd like that makes when everyone is cheering, stamping, and thundering at the same time. I was only one person in that sea of people, but for a few hours that day, we were all one, witnessing American history being made. I was given an exclusive peek into the heart of the human spirit that day. It is something that will stay with me for the rest of my life.

Presidential Recognition

After I wrote my account of the trip to the inauguration, I sent a copy to President Barack Obama along with a cover letter. In March, 2011, I was extremely excited to receive mail from The White House, and find that the President had written me in reply!

Below are the letter I received from President Obama and the cover letter I sent to him along with my story:

Anita Coggs Rowell
November 29, 2010

Dear President Obama,

"The Trip of a Lifetime: Traveling with My Father to the Presidential Inauguration of Barack Obama" is the story I wrote after attending your historic inauguration with my Tuskegee Airman father.

It was such a tremendous honor and privilege for him and all the other Airmen to receive an invitation from you to attend the inauguration.

In some ways you and my father share commonalities: both of you have graduated from Harvard University. My father, Dr. Granville Coggs, is of the class of 1953, Harvard Medical School; and each of you has two daughters.

I had never traveled with just my father before, so you can appreciate how our first father-daughter road trip - having the opportunity to attend your inauguration – was an unforgettable experience and definitely the trip of a lifetime for both of us.

Since I am quite aware that you have many "thorns" on your plate right now, I decided to send you my story, since I thought you might enjoy reading about a positive, inspirational and hopeful time in our lives that you created. It could also give you a chance to smell the "roses".

Writing to you gives me the chance to thank you for your service to our country and for persevering in the face of so much adversity.

Sincerely,
Anita Coggs Rowell

THE WHITE HOUSE

WASHINGTON

March 1, 2011

Ms. Anita Coggs Rowell
2139 Vintage Circle
Santa Rosa, California 95404

Dear Anita:

Thank you for taking the time to write. I have heard many personal accounts from individuals and families across our country, and I appreciate your sharing your story with me.

Each day, I read letters from Americans so that I stay connected to their real-life and diverse experiences. By working together and involving all Americans in shaping the policies that affect us, we will build a brighter future for ourselves and our Nation.

Thank you again for sharing your story with me. I wish you all the best in the future.

Sincerely,

Meanwhile, Back at the Ranch

The filmmaker, George Lucas, recently released a movie about the Tuskegee Airmen called "Red Tails." Tracy Cannobbio, the chief publicist for Lucasfilm, invited me to the Skywalker Ranch and gave us a tour. Anita also captured our visit in writing:

Meanwhile, Back at the Ranch by Anita Coggs Rowell

After we waited briefly at the entrance to the Skywalker Ranch in west Marin County, a metal gate swung open, and we were in. We weren't sure what to expect, since Lucasfilm was extremely secretive about the Ranch. Making our way to the Security Kiosk, we took in the lush landscape. Clusters of rosemary bushes dotted the sides of the roadway. Green rolling hills were covered with the latticework of olive groves. Rows of vineyards were decorated with the rustling glints of bright orange, crimson, and deep yellow hues in the golden sunlight. We were met at the Security Kiosk by our guide, Tracy Cannobbio, who is the publicist for Lucasfilm.

Granville and Tracy Cannobbio

"Red Tails" is a completed feature-length tribute to the Tuskegee Airmen set for release January 20, 2012. Other Tuskegee Airmen have been out to the Ranch, and on this beautiful fall afternoon, November 29, 2011, my father had been invited to come to the Ranch, along with his guests. My husband, Joe, and I were my dad's guests, and Tracy gave the three of us a two-hour tour of the property.

As we drove to Skywalker Sound, we passed a large barn, a garden with raised beds, and crossed a covered bridge. We went by the

Main House

softball diamond and the horses grazing in their corral. Adding to the bucolic surroundings was a herd of cows ambling about at the ridge of the hills. On our way, we kept saying, "Wow!... Look at that!... Ah, that's beautiful...."

Anita, Granville, and Joe

I didn't take notes on the tour, although I knew I'd be writing about it. I felt that carrying a note pad and jotting down information as we went along wouldn't be a good idea.

After passing a picturesque lake we arrived at the Technical Building which houses Skywalker Sound. The building's craftsman style architecture incorporated stone, wood, and brick. At the door we were greeted by John Greber, the building manager.

The ambiance inside the Technical Building had a warm, comfortable feeling. The walls were lined with classic posters and we passed corridors leading to offices. Lots of light and wooden furniture upholstered in soft colors filled rooms for lounging and dining.

John proceeded to lead us to the Stag Theater. The theater was a 300 seat state-of-the art screening room; its Art Deco architecture was beautiful, based on the design of George Lucas' favorite movie theater in his hometown of Modesto. Although there were plush seats and soft carpeting in the theater, the most noteworthy attribute was the absolute silence that enveloped us. Even with the four of us walking around inside the theater, there was an amazing hush. Our footsteps made no sound. The acoustics in that theater were impeccable. Tracy told us that we were standing "in the best theater on the planet!" I could believe it.

Tracy explained that other directors have used the facilities at Skywalker Sound for post-production audio. "Some of George's friends, like Clint Eastwood, and Steven Spielberg have been here."

'Right', I thought to myself. 'Of course, friends of George are guys like Clint and Steven.'

"As a matter of fact, Oprah was just here last week," she continued.

"Really?" I exclaimed. "Where did she sit?"

Tracy pointed to a spot near the last row of seats at the top, "Right there."

"She was real nice," Tracy added.

"I would think so," I replied.

After we sat down, we got a demo of post-production sound mixing. We watched a scene from Saving Private Ryan being screened, starting with the first rough cut, then listening to the incremental layers of sound being added, finishing with the final version shown in the movie. The Sensurround came from all over the theater. If there was an explosion or cannons were fired, the intensity of the sound made it feel like the floor was shaking. It was fascinating.

After walking out to the front porch and veranda, there was a sweeping view of the vineyards and lake. Benches on the porch were arranged to take in the scenery. In the distance at the foot of the hills, among the trees, we could see the Main House, a large white house with Victorian architecture.

As we looked at the Main House, Tracy said, "Well, I guess you heard about the fire at the Main House recently."

Joe and I said we knew about it since the fire at the Ranch had been on the news. She went on to say that since the repairs to the Main House weren't completed yet, we wouldn't be able to see it on our tour.

"You know you're welcome to come back anytime," she told us, "so you'll just have to see it on your next visit."

In my head, my jaw dropped, as I recognized that we had just been invited to return to the Ranch.

My dad said, "Well, thank you, we look forward to seeing it."

We commented on the peaceful setting of the landscape, which was stunning in the sunlight that autumn afternoon.

Tracy explained that when George Lucas built Skywalker Ranch, he wanted to get away from L.A., and establish a place in Northern California where the staff could work in an environment that would foster creativity and productivity.

Clearly, that was accomplished. This would be a great place to

:ome to work.

"We're going to the Archives next," Tracy told us. Then she nentioned, "Many people on the staff here have never been inside." So, ve were very grateful for our opportunity to tour it. The Archives were ıoused in a building constructed like a big, blue, two-story barn.

Inside, we were met by two wardrobe archivists. For :onfidentiality, I will refer to them here as Janice and Sarah. They showed ıs around the huge warehouse where all the costumes for Star Wars, and he Indiana Jones movies were kept, and it was amazing to see so many :ostumes displayed on the mannequins. There were movable aisles filled vith row after row of costumes, as well as shoes and hats on shelves.

It had been a long time since I'd seen Star Wars, but I had lecided to watch it when it came on the Syfy Channel Sunday afternoon, November 27th. This turned out to be a good thing because many of the :haracters and the plot were still fresh in my mind.

We looked at some of the costumes that the actors wore in Red Tails, where there were rows of bomber jackets. It was surprising that he parachute harness the Airmen had worn was so heavy--it must have veighed at least thirty pounds.

We found R2D2 standing on his rolling pedestal; he certainly was :ute.

The same was true for C-3PO. That day the metal panel on part of ıis torso had been removed, exposing his wiring grid.

Darth Vader's costume was very large, black, and foreboding. We ıadn't realized how big and tall the actor who wore it must have been.

Chewie was in a group with a couple of his tall, furry friends and . little Wookie pup. Nearby was Luke Skywalker's orange flight suit.

I admired a beautiful vermillion gown embellished with gold :mbroidery and fur trim. Attached to the gown was a crown surrounded ›y a sweeping hairstyle. This costume was worn by Natalie Portman as Queen Padme Amidala in "Star Wars: Episode I – The Phantom Menace."

A jacket Michael Jackson had worn was hanging on a rack. Its lesign had quilted white leather, studded forearms and shoulders, and :olorful jewel detailing along the lapels. Looking at the width of the houlders, I was struck by how slight his build had been.

Queen Amidala and Anita

Anita and R2D2

Granville, Luke Skywalker, and Joe

Granville, Michael Jackson's jacket, Anita

Darth Maul, Joe, Anita, Darth Vader, Granville

Granville holding a Red Tail's bomber jacket

Anita, C-3PO, Granville

Sarah and Janice were very informative and interesting as they showed us around. When we came to the Indiana Jones section, we looked at the jackets and shoes that Indy had worn. Sarah was telling us about them, and then she hesitated.

She said, "Here, why don't we try something?" and looked at my father. She took a leather jacket off its hanger and went over to him.

"I've never done this before," she told him, "but it just seems like you should wear this."

Janice gave Sarah an incredulous look, and reaffirmed, "She's never done that before!"

She helped him put on the jacket, checked out how he looked, and then turned around to pick up a box. She took a fedora out of the box. Yes, it was "the hat." Here was the hat that Indy always wore--the hat that was so important for him to keep track of during his adventures. She handed him the hat and he put it on.

Sarah stepped back to see how my dad looked, seemed pleased and said, "There!"

My father smiled and showed off the hat and jacket.

"Unbelievable!" I said. "Get a shot of this!"

Granville wearing Indiana Jones' jacket and hat

After we were finished with that section, we thanked Janice and Sarah and left the Archives. In the front we thanked Tracy for our tour and told her goodbye.

From the time we drove out of the gate and until we got home, we talked about our extraordinary afternoon. Joe and I thanked my dad for making it possible for us to have such an unforgettable experience. I've had fun just remembering and writing about our visit. Perhaps there will be a sequel to this account should we end up back at the ranch.

Anita Rowell December 31, 2011

The End

Made in the USA
Charleston, SC
18 February 2013